# The Last of The Mohicans

by James Fenimore Cooper

Abridged and adapted by John M. Hurdy

Illustrated by Jane Larson

A PACEMAKER CLASSIC

FEARON / JANUS / QUERCUS
Belmont, California

Simon & Schuster Education Group

## Other Pacemaker Classics

*The Adventures of Huckleberry Finn*
*The Adventures of Tom Sawyer*
*A Christmas Carol*
*Crime and Punishment*
*The Deerslayer*
*Dr. Jekyll and Mr. Hyde*
*Ethan Frome*
*Frankenstein*
*Great Expectations*
*Jane Eyre*
*The Jungle Book*
*Moby Dick*
*The Moonstone*
*The Red Badge of Courage*
*Robinson Crusoe*
*The Scarlet Letter*
*A Tale of Two Cities*
*The Three Musketeers*
*The Time Machine*
*Treasure Island*
*20,000 Leagues Under the Sea*
*Two Years Before the Mast*
*Wuthering Heights*

ISBN 0–8224–9215–6
Library of Congress Card Number: 67–25787

Printed in the United States of America.

2. 12 11 10 9 8 7 6 5 4 3
MA

# Contents

1   Going to Fort William Henry . . 1

2   Lost in the Woods . . . . . . 8

3   The Attack . . . . . . . . 14

4   Magua . . . . . . . . . 27

5   Through the French Lines . . . 39

6   A Red Coat . . . . . . . . 47

7   On the Trail . . . . . . . . 56

8   The Bear . . . . . . . . 66

9   A Trick . . . . . . . . . 73

10   The Last of the Mohicans . . . 83

# 1 Going to Fort William Henry

The time was 1757. The English and the French were fighting each other in America. Each country wanted to own all of America.

In 1757, America was still very wild. There were few towns and not many farms in the country. There were some open fields. But most of the land was covered with dark woods. In some places there were so many trees that you could not see the sky. Only Indians and wild animals could go through the woods without getting lost.

The people who lived in the English part of America loved the land. They were trying to make homes in the woods for their families. They grew food for their families on little farms. It was hard work. But they wanted to live in America so much they did not care.

Farmers do not fight well. They must use their time to take care of their farms. They do not have the time to learn how to fight. But the French sent soldiers and Indian tribes to fight the English farmers in America. Many of the farmers were killed. So the English sent their own soldiers to fight the French soldiers.

*1*

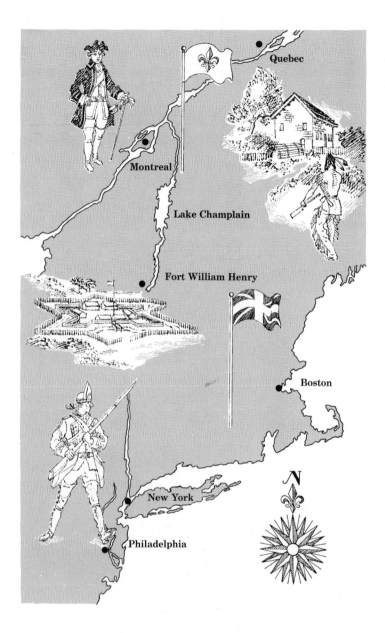

Quebec

Montreal

Lake Champlain

Fort William Henry

Boston

New York

Philadelphia

N

That is why Cora and Alice Munro came from England. Their father, Colonel Munro, was an English soldier. Cora had dark hair and brown eyes. Alice had blue eyes and light hair. Some people thought Cora was more beautiful than Alice. Other people thought Alice was more beautiful than Cora. But it did not matter, because they were both beautiful. And they were as nice to be with as they were pretty.

The two sisters could have stayed in England away from the fighting. There they could have gone to parties and shopped for new clothes. But their father was a soldier. When he was sent to America, Cora and Alice came with him.

Colonel Munro commanded the English soldiers at Fort William Henry. There were not many soldiers at Fort William Henry. That was bad at any time. But then word came that the French were on the move. They were bringing up "as many men as there are leaves on the trees." They were coming to try to take Fort William Henry.

The French were willing to do anything to win. They got the Huron and the Delaware Indians to help them. They gave these Indians many presents to kill the English. This was very bad for the farmers, because Indians did not fight like soldiers. They killed not only men, but women and children, too. At night they would make a surprise attack on a farmer's house. Sometimes the Indians would kill only one of the family. At other times, no one was left when the Indians were through.

Cora and Alice had been visiting some friends many miles from Fort William Henry. Then they heard that the French were coming. They wanted to go to their father's side.

But how could they get home? Fort William Henry was a long ride away. The girls could not go alone.

Major Duncan Heyward was a soldier under Colonel Munro's command. He was going back to Fort William Henry. He said he would take the girls back with him.

In those days English soldiers had coats of bright red. That was why they were called Redcoats. Major Heyward had on a bright red coat, too. But he was better looking than most soldiers.

Major Heyward liked both girls, but he loved Alice. He found two good horses for Cora and Alice to ride. And he brought along his Indian scout, Magua, to show them the way.

Magua had a tomahawk and a scalping knife. His face was covered with colored paints. But still, Magua did not look like most Indians.

Just as the four of them were about to start off, a man rode up. He was thin, and so was his horse. His clothes were too short for him. And he was too long for his horse. He did not ride his horse well. In short, he looked like a clown in the circus riding a circus horse.

The girls, who were very kind, tried hard not to laugh.

"Who are you?" Major Heyward asked.

"I, my good man, am a singing teacher," answered the thin man.

"A singing teacher!" Major Heyward could not believe his ears.

The thin man said, "That is right. I teach people how to sing."

"Anyone knows how to sing," said Major Heyward. "What is your work?"

"I teach people how to sing," said the thin man. "That is enough to do."

Major Heyward did not like that answer. He thought that with a war going on a man should do more than teach singing.

"May I ride with you?" asked the singing teacher. He sounded afraid. "I want to go to Fort William Henry. But the woods are full of Indians and I do not know how to fight."

Major Heyward did not want to have to take

care of a singing teacher. It was enough to watch out for two girls. But Alice liked singing.

"Let him come with us, Duncan," she said.

Major Heyward could never say no to Alice.

"I will sing a song for you, my dear," said the singing teacher to Alice. He said this as though he were giving her a present.

They had not gone far when Major Heyward cried, "What was that?" He pulled his horse to a stop. He thought he had seen a face through the branches of a tree.

Magua rode back to the Major. "Come," Magua said. "No time to stop."

"No," said Major Heyward. "I saw something behind those trees." He looked into the woods.

"Do you think you could see something I could not?" Magua laughed. "Indian eyes are better than white eyes. There is nothing in the trees but birds."

But Magua was lying. After Major Heyward's party rode on, an Indian stepped out from the trees. He was a Huron, and he was painted for war. The Huron took careful note of the trail the party was taking.

Magua knew the Hurons were watching them. But he did not know the woods held three other men.

# 2 Lost in the Woods

One of the three other men in the woods was a white man. His name was Hawkeye. He was a scout for the English.

Hawkeye was tall and thin. He was wearing clothes made from the skins of deer. The sun had browned his face. And time had put a little gray in his hair. But he was very strong. And he knew as much about the woods as any Indian. He had always lived in the woods.

The other two men were Indians. But they were not Hurons. They were the last two men left of a great tribe of Indians. Chingachgook and his son, Uncas, were the last of the Mohicans.

The Mohicans were painted all over. They did not wear many clothes. And on their heads they had just one long band of hair. This band was for their enemies to scalp—if they could. They had tied feathers into their hair.

Chingachgook was sitting on a log. Near him was a dead deer that Uncas had shot. Hawkeye was filling his powder horn.

Hawkeye and his Indian friends were not surprised when Major Heyward's party rode up. Uncas had heard them from far off. He had put his ear to the ground. He could tell five horses were coming.

"Who are you?" Hawkeye called. He threw his rifle over his left arm. He was ready for anything.

The singing teacher was riding in front of the others. "We are English," he answered. "We have been riding all day. And we are lost."

Then Major Heyward came riding up. "Which way is it to Fort William Henry?" he asked.

"If it is William Henry you want," Hawkeye said, "you *are* lost. You should not have tried to find your way through the woods alone."

"We are not alone," said Major Heyward. "An Indian is showing us the way. But he says he is lost."

"An Indian lost!" Hawkeye laughed. "I find that hard to believe. Are you sure he is not working for the French?"

Major Heyward sat up very straight. "I know that man," he said. "He is a Mohawk. They are friends of the English."

Hawkeye laughed again. "You are not sure of him now. Your voice gives you away. Let me have a look at him."

*9*

Hawkeye ran down the trail. He ran as fast as an Indian. Around a turn in the trail, he stopped and hid. He saw Cora and Alice for the first time. The sisters were talking to each other while they waited. Behind them, with his back against a tree, stood Magua.

One look was enough for Hawkeye. He ran back to Major Heyward.

"I was right," Hawkeye said. "Your scout is a Huron. He may have lived with the Mohawks for a while. But once a Huron, always a Huron. It is a wonder you still have your scalps."

"Do you think so?" asked Major Heyward, quieting his horse. "I did think it funny that he lost his way. What shall I do now?"

"Go to him and keep him talking," said Hawkeye. "Uncas and Chingachgook will take him from behind."

The sun was going down. The woods were growing very dark. If the Hurons were going to attack, they would do it soon. It was the time Indians liked to attack.

Major Heyward rode his horse back down the trail. He gave Cora and Alice a warm smile as he went by them. He was glad to see they did not know they were in danger.

Magua was still standing with his back against

the tree. Major Heyward rode up to him. "Everything is going to be all right," he said. "I came across a man who knows where we are. He is up the trail. He will take us to Fort William Henry."

Magua's eyes had a new and fierce light in them. "Is this man alone?" he asked.

Major Heyward did not want Magua to know about Uncas and Chingachgook. But the Major

was not very good at lying. "No," he said. "We are with him now."

His answer made Magua feel that something was going on. "I will go," Magua said in a cold voice. "Then the white men will see only their own color."

"Now, Magua," said Major Heyward, "what will Colonel Munro think if you go? He will give you a fine present when you bring his children. There is no need to be angry. Everything is going to be all right. You must be tired. Get some rest and have something to eat."

The Indian sat down on the ground. He took his food bag from around his neck. But he was wondering if Major Heyward had found out he was lying.

Major Heyward wanted to catch Magua himself. He got off his horse and went up to the Huron. "What do you have to eat?" he asked. "Here. Let me give you some of my food."

Magua handed him his food bag. But when Major Heyward moved his hand toward his arm, Magua ran into the woods.

At the same time, Chingachgook ran out from behind some trees. He took off after the Huron. Uncas followed.

Then Hawkeye's rifle fired.

# 3 The Attack

Blood spotted the ground where Magua had been running. Hawkeye had hit his man. But the Huron got away into the woods. Chingachgook and Uncas could not catch him. Major Heyward wanted to go after him.

"No!" said Hawkeye, holding him back. "Follow him and you will find his tribe down your neck. By tomorrow your scalp would be drying in the wind."

"But he is wounded," cried Major Heyward.

"Not much," said Hawkeye. "From where I stood it was a good shot. But it did not go deep. He is more angry than hurt."

Major Heyward did not know what to do. "If I don't go after Magua," he said, "he will bring more Hurons. We must think of the ladies. Help us and you can have as much money as you want."

Hawkeye gave Major Heyward a cold look. "Don't talk to me about money, or to my friends. We will do what we can for the two young ladies. But you must give us your word about something."

*14*

"About what?" asked Major Heyward.

"No matter what happens," said Hawkeye, "don't make any noise. And never tell anyone about the place to which we take you."

"On my word, we will do as you wish," Major Heyward said.

"Good," said Hawkeye. "Now hurry. We must get moving."

Major Heyward went over to Cora and Alice. He told them how Magua had tried to trick them. He told them that Hawkeye would help them if they did as he said.

Cora and Alice were afraid. But they smiled and said they would do their best.

Hawkeye knew the Hurons would come looking for the girls. He wanted Magua to think Heyward's party had run off. Then Magua would go looking for them in another part of the woods.

The horses would give them away if the Indians saw them. Magua knew the girls could not go far without their horses. So, Uncas and Chingachgook hid the horses. There was a river not far away. They took them down into the river where they would not make a trail. Then they tied them to a tree and left them standing in the water.

Hawkeye took Heyward and the others down to the river. Soon they came to the place where he kept his canoe. Heyward helped him put the canoe into the river. The water was cold and ran fast. It almost knocked the two men off their feet. They held the canoe while the girls climbed in. Then they pushed the canoe up the river. The singing teacher followed them.

After a short time, they came to a turn in the river. There they saw a very high and very wide waterfall. The water seemed to be coming down from the sky. It fell into the river with a loud roaring noise.

At a sign from Hawkeye, the men climbed into the canoe. Then Hawkeye headed the canoe right into the angry waters coming from the waterfall.

Water splashed all around them. The light canoe was pushed first one way and then another. The noise grew so loud that Alice felt sure they would be killed. She covered her eyes with her hands. When she looked again, she saw an island. "Where are we?" she asked.

"We are at the foot of Glenn's Falls," Hawkeye answered. "Sit still while I land the canoe. The water runs fast here. If you fall in, you will be carried away before we can save you."

Hawkeye landed the canoe on the island. He and Major Heyward helped the others out of the canoe. "Now I will go bring in Uncas and Chingachgook," he said.

Soon Hawkeye came back to the island with the two Indians. Then he showed them the way into a long, dark cave. Once in the cave, Hawkeye made a fire. Then he began cooking the meat of the deer Uncas had killed that day.

Cora and Alice sat by the fire to warm their hands. By the light of the fire, they looked at the men who had helped them.

Alice was afraid of Indians. But there was something about Uncas that was not like other Indians. He looked kind as well as strong. He seemed to be good as well as brave. And he was very good looking.

"With a man like Uncas for a friend," said Alice, "we need not be afraid."

"Yes," Duncan Heyward answered. "The Mohican seems to be a good man."

Hawkeye looked up. "Dinner is ready," he said. "This is not the kind of food you are used to. But it is the best we can do."

"Should we stay in this cave?" asked Duncan. "Could the Hurons take us here by surprise?"

"Chingachgook and I are old foxes," said

Hawkeye. "We do not get into a hole with only one way out. Once this island was one large rock. But the river worked this hole for us to hide in. The waterfall is on both sides of us. The river runs behind us and in front of us. We will be all right here."

Uncas handed food and water to Cora and Alice. The young Mohican's English was not good. But his voice was deep and pleasing. He was helping both girls. But he took a little better care of Cora. And he could not keep his eyes off her face.

Heyward could not help smiling to himself. He knew that Indians were not used to waiting on girls. Indian girls waited on their men and ate after the men were finished.

Chingachgook sat and ate without saying a word. He looked much like his son. Now that he was with friends, he did not look fierce.

Hawkeye never seemed to rest. He would stop eating to listen. He would stop listening to look. He kept close watch on both ends of the cave. Once his eyes fell on the singing teacher.

"Come, friend," he said. "Have some water. It will wash away bad times. What is your name?"

"Gamut—David Gamut," the thin man said.

"What do you do for a living?" Hawkeye asked.

David took a deep drink of water. When he finished, he said, "I teach singing."

"Do you know how to use a rifle?" Hawkeye asked.

"Thanks be to God, no!" said David.

Hawkeye tried to cover a laugh. "It is a funny way to live. To go about like a bird while other men work."

All at once, from outside the cave came the sound of wild cries. David jumped up and ran to the mouth of the cave. Hawkeye called him back and went after him. But it was too late. There was the noise of many rifles firing. David fell to the ground. He had been hit in the head.

Hawkeye's long rifle answered the shots. On the other side of the river, a Huron cried out. Then the cries and rifle fire stopped.

Duncan Heyward ran to David and carried him back into the cave.

"Can I help?" asked Cora. "Is he dead?"

Hawkeye came back and looked at the wound. "No," he said. "The wound is not deep. Let him be. He is of no use to us. Singing will not drive the Hurons away."

"But they stopped," Duncan said. "Do you think they will attack again?"

Hawkeye laughed. "They lost a man. That was why they fell back. But they will come again. With the Hurons you may be sure of that. They must have come up the river and seen the horses."

Uncas and Chingachgook hid along the sides of the small island. Hawkeye and Duncan stayed near the mouth of the cave. It was a long watch in a cold, dark night.

Duncan began to think again that the Hurons had gone away. He said as much to Hawkeye as the sun came up.

Hawkeye answered with a quick shake of his head. "They know how few we are. They want our scalps. My guess is that they will try to get to this island from behind. They will come over the waterfall. Keep your eyes open or your hair will be lost."

Duncan kept his eyes on the waterfall. Hawkeye was right! Five Indians were coming down the waterfall toward the island. As they watched, one of the Indians was caught up by the fast-moving waters. They could see the Huron fighting to stay on top of the water. But the water was too strong for him. In a minute, he was carried under and seen no more. But the other four made it to the island.

"Hurons!" Uncas yelled.

"I see them, boy," Hawkeye called. "They will attack any minute," he told Duncan. "Be ready."

Just then, the four Hurons raced toward them. Hawkeye brought one of them down. Uncas got another. Duncan fired at the same time, but he missed.

The last two Hurons came running for the cave.

"Come on!" yelled Hawkeye. He jumped at one of the Indians with his knife. Duncan went after the other.

Hand-to-hand fighting was old work for Hawkeye. But Duncan was having a hard time of it. His Huron was very strong. He and Duncan rolled over and over on the rocks. The Indian's hands had found Duncan's neck. He was pressing hard on Duncan's neck. Just then, a knife flew into the Indian's back. The Huron fell over dead. Uncas had saved Duncan.

"Take cover!" yelled Hawkeye. "Get behind some rocks. Our work is not finished."

Rifle fire came from across the river. Chingachgook and Uncas gave the Hurons back shot for shot.

"Don't fire," cried Hawkeye. "I have used the last of my powder. Better go to the canoe and get the big powder horn, Uncas. If I know Hurons, we will need every drop of it."

The young Mohican ran to the canoe, but he was too late. A Huron had found the canoe. Uncas could see him swimming with it to the other side of the river. When he got to dry land, he let out a great yell.

"They have something to yell about," Hawkeye said. "The best rifle in the world can not fire without powder."

"What can we do?" asked Duncan.

Hawkeye did not answer in so many words. His hand went to his hair in a way that said everything.

"It can not be that bad," Duncan said. "We can fight them."

"With what?" asked Hawkeye. "Uncas' arrows? Against their rifles?"

Chingachgook sat very still. He took the feather from his hair. Beside him he placed his knife and his tomahawk. His time to be scalped had come. "Uncas," he said, "you are a Mohican. A chief and the son of a chief. Our people were the best of the Delawares. We must show the Hurons that the last of the Mohicans are brave."

"No!" cried Cora as she ran to them from the cave. "You must not stay and be killed. You can get away. Swim down the river. Hide in the woods."

Hawkeye turned to her and smiled. "Knowing we had left you to the Hurons? You are a brave girl, but that will not do. It would be better to be killed. What could I say to your father?"

"Don't you see?" Cora said. She took Hawkeye's arm. "Go to my father. Tell him to come with his men. If he hurries, there may still be time."

Hawkeye tried not to listen. But he knew Cora was right. Without powder, they were of no use to the girls on the island. If they got away, there might be something they could do.

"What do you think, Chingachgook? Uncas?" he asked. "Did you hear the dark-haired woman?"

Hawkeye held Cora's hand. "You are right, young lady," he said. "I wish it were not so. We will go. You must try to hide from them. Play for time. If they catch you, leave a trail. No matter what happens, we will come after you."

Hawkeye, Chingachgook, and Uncas ran to the river and jumped into its dark waters.

Cora looked at Duncan. "I know you can swim," she said.

"Cora Munro," Duncan answered. "No matter what you say, I am staying here. I will not go without you. And that is that."

# 4 Magua

Now Duncan, Cora, Alice, and David were alone on the island. There was no sign of Hawkeye or the Mohicans. Duncan was not even sure they had not been killed by the wild river.

"I don't see the Hurons now," he said, looking across into the woods.

The singing teacher still did not know what had happened to him. He could sit up, but he could not think. Duncan would not get any help from him.

Duncan began throwing branches in front of the cave. He hoped that the branches would keep the Hurons from finding the cave.

Duncan had almost covered the mouth of the cave. Just then, David gave a funny smile and began singing.

"Should we let him sing?" Cora asked. "The Hurons might hear him."

"Not above the noise of the waterfall," Duncan answered. "Let him sing. It may make him feel better."

But a yell from outside the cave cut David short. The Hurons were on the island!

"They have found us!" cried Alice.

"No," Duncan said in a quiet voice. "They are on the island, but they have not found us. There is still hope."

Another wild yell followed the first. Duncan could hear the Hurons racing across the island looking for them. As the Indians ran, they were yelling, "Hawkeye! Hawkeye!" The word went from mouth to mouth as they looked for their hated enemy.

Two Indians came near the hiding place. They even bumped into the branches that hid the cave. Duncan could see their feet through the leaves. But the branches did their work. The Indians did not see the cave. After a short time, they left.

"They are gone, Cora!" Duncan said. "Alice, we are saved!"

Alice opened her eyes and started to smile. But then her face went white. She cried out and pointed to something behind Duncan.

It was Magua, the bad Indian scout. He had come in through the cave's other opening. He stood there watching them. His face was filled with hate.

Duncan fired his rifle at Magua. He missed. Before he could fire again, the rest of the Hurons came running in. They dragged Duncan and the others out of the cave.

Magua pointed to where Hawkeye had wounded him. "Where is the one who did this?" he asked. "He is a white man but he knows the trails through the woods. He fights like an Indian, but he could not kill Magua." Then he laughed in Duncan's face. "And," he went on, "the rifle of the white soldier could not even hit Magua."

Duncan wanted to hit Magua in the face. But he had to think of the girls. He said, "Magua is too great to think about the wounds he gets in war."

The Hurons were still yelling Hawkeye's name.

"You hear?" Magua asked. "My people want Hawkeye's scalp."

"Hawkeye is not here," Duncan said.

Magua pressed his knife against Duncan's face near his eye. "Tell me where Hawkeye is!" he said.

"He has gone," Duncan said again.

"Is he a bird that he can fly?" Magua roared. "Or did he swim down the river like a fish? Just because the white soldier can read, he thinks Indians know nothing."

"Hawkeye is no fish," said Duncan. "But he can swim. He had used up all his rifle powder. Why should he stay?"

"Then why did the white soldier stay?" asked Magua. "Does his scalp want to come off?"

"The ladies can not swim," Duncan answered. "And I would not let them stay here alone."

Magua seemed to believe Duncan. "And the Mohicans?" he asked. "Did they go down the river, too?"

"Yes," Duncan said.

When the Hurons found out that Hawkeye was gone, they went wild. One of them grabbed Alice by the hair. Duncan jumped at the Indian. But he was knocked down and his hands were tied.

The Huron brave holding Alice took out his knife. He made as if he were going to scalp her. Magua watched, laughing.

After a while, Magua grew tired of this game. "We go!" he yelled to the other Hurons.

The Indians took their captives across the river. They got the five horses that Uncas and Chingachgook hid in the river. Then most of the Huron war party headed north with three of the horses. Five braves stayed behind with Magua and the captives. The two horses they had were for the girls.

Duncan helped Alice and Cora to get on their horses. He walked beside them as they rode west along the trail. They were watched from each side by two Indians. The Indians stayed close to them all the time.

Following Hawkeye's plan, Cora was trying to leave a trail. She would ride her horse close to trees along the way. Then she would break off some of the leaves. She hoped Hawkeye would see them. Once she even dropped one of her rings. But the Hurons saw her each time. They picked up the leaves and her ring.

It was late afternoon when Magua made them climb up a small hill. Once at the top, Magua threw himself down on the ground. At last they were going to rest. David was quite sick from all the walking. And even Duncan was tired. It had been a long, long march.

After a while, one of the Indians went out hunting. He came back with a young deer. Soon the five Hurons were eating. They ate the meat of the dead deer without cooking it. Just watching them made Alice feel sick.

Magua did not eat with the other Indians. He sat alone under a tree. His fierce face was dark with hate. "Bring me the dark-haired one!" he yelled to Duncan.

Duncan went and brought back Cora. On the way he told her, "Try to keep your head. I

32

know you will. You are brave, just like your father."

Magua stood looking at Cora for some minutes without saying anything. Then he made a sign with his hand for Duncan to go away.

At first Duncan would not go. But Cora said in a soft voice, "Please go. We had better do as he wants." Then she turned to the Indian. "Yes?" she asked.

Magua put his hand on her arm. "Magua is a chief of the Hurons," he said. "Before he saw the white man he was happy. Then the French came into our woods and gave Magua fire-water. Magua became a bad Indian. He did anything to get fire-water. His people made him go away from the land of his fathers. Can Magua help it if his head is not made of rock? Who gave him the fire-water? It was people of your own color."

Cora pulled her arm away. "There are bad white men just as there are bad Indians," she said. "This is not my doing."

"Listen!" said Magua. "When the English and the French made war, I went with the English. I began fighting my own people. The old chief, your father, was the head of my war party. He said he would whip any Indian he found drinking fire-water. But Magua could not keep away from the fire-water. And what did the Gray-head do to him? Let his child say."

"My father kept his word," Cora said. She looked straight into the Indian's angry eyes.

"The word was bad!" Magua yelled. "Magua could not help himself. He had to drink the fire-water. But the Gray-head would not believe him. He had his soldiers whip Magua like a dog."

Pointing to an old wound on his arm, he said, "Look! When my enemy cut me here, I laughed. I told him only a woman could give such a little cut. But the blows of Munro are still hurting me."

Cora was afraid. "What do you want?" she asked.

"What a Huron loves," Magua answered. "Good for good. Bad for bad."

"Would you get even with a man through his children?" Cora asked. "Would it not be more like a man to meet my father face to face?"

Magua laughed. "And be killed by the rifles of the Gray-head's soldiers?"

"What are you going to do?" asked Cora.

"When Magua left his people, he lost his woman. She went to another chief. Magua needs a woman. Let the child of the great white chief live in Magua's tent. You shall be my woman!"

These words made Cora feel sick. Her ears buzzed. For a minute she could not see. It was all she could do to stay on her feet. "Does the chief wish to have a woman he does not love?" she asked. "It would be better to take money from my father. With that you could buy presents for a woman of your own people."

Magua smiled at Cora. It was the smile of a fox, filled with hate. Cora could not bear to look at him.

"No," said Magua. "Munro's child will draw Magua's water. She will carry his things. She will cook his food. And when Magua's old wounds hurt, he will know where to find Munro's child."

"You animal!" cried Cora.

Magua waved her away. Cora left almost at a run.

Duncan hurried over to her. He could see that she was both angry and afraid. "What happened?" he asked.

But Cora did not want Alice to know about Magua's plans. Shaking her head, she said nothing.

Magua had gone over to the other five Hurons. Their hands were still red with blood from the deer meat. But they had finished eating.

Magua began talking, using his hands as much as his mouth. He pointed to the girls. He made signs. He roared. In a few minutes, he had them ready to do anything he wanted.

Then Magua gave a command. The Hurons jumped up and ran yelling toward the girls.

Duncan threw himself in front of the girls. But two Indians pulled him away and tied him to one of the trees. They tied David to another tree. Then the Hurons grabbed Cora and Alice and tied each of them to a tree.

Alice was crying. Only the ropes kept her from falling down. Cora was afraid, too. But she held herself up straight and would not cry.

"What says the child of Munro now?" asked Magua. "Is she still too good for Magua?"

"What is he talking about?" asked Duncan, pulling against his ropes.

"Nothing," said Cora. "The man is an animal. He does not know what he is doing."

"I know," said Magua, in an angry voice. "Shall I send the yellow-haired one to her father? Will you carry Magua's water and feed him corn?"

Cora closed her eyes. She wished she could close her ears, too. "Go away!" she cried.

Magua pointed to Alice. "Look!" he said. "She is too young to be killed. Send her to Munro."

Cora could not help looking at her sister. The Indian's words had filled Alice with hope. "Is he going to send me home?" she asked.

Cora looked at her sister for a long time. At last she found the words she needed. "Alice," she said, "Magua will not kill you if I stay here with him. He wants me for his woman. Shall I stay, Alice?"

"How could you ask such a thing?" Alice cried. "I could not live knowing you were with him. It is better for us to be killed together."

With a fierce cry of hate, Magua threw his tomahawk at Alice. It hit close to her head, cutting off some of her hair.

That was too much for Duncan. He pulled against his ropes, breaking them. Another Indian was about to throw a knife at Alice. Duncan caught his arm just in time. They fell to the ground, the Indian landing on top of Duncan. His knife pressed down toward Duncan's neck. Duncan could feel its point against his skin.

All at once, there was the sound of a rifle shot. The Indian on top of Duncan fell over dead.

# 5 Through the French Lines

The Hurons stood with their mouths open. They could not believe what they saw with their own eyes. They knew only one man could have made such a shot. "Hawkeye!" they cried.

With an answering yell, Hawkeye raced out from behind a tree. He had not waited to put more powder in his rifle. He ran swinging the rifle over his head.

Uncas ran out and attacked the Hurons who were holding Cora. Knife in hand, Chingachgook was not far behind.

Magua grabbed his scalping knife and went after Chingachgook. Duncan pulled the tomahawk from the tree where Alice was tied. He had never used one before. But his first throw caught a Huron in the face.

The fighting was fast and fierce. Uncas opened up a Huron's head with one fierce blow. Duncan jumped another Indian. Duncan knew he could not hold on long. But he did not have to. Hawkeye's rifle came swinging down on the Indian's head, killing him.

One of the Hurons threw his tomahawk at Cora. It hit the ropes around her and cut through them. Cora ran to her sister. But before she could get to Alice, the Huron caught her. Pushing her to the ground, he held up his scalping knife.

Uncas looked up in time to see Cora's danger. He jumped, feet first, knocking the Huron down. But Uncas fell, too. Duncan's tomahawk and Hawkeye's shot hit the Huron at the same time. The Huron was dead before Uncas got to his feet.

Chingachgook and Magua were still fighting. Covered with blood, they rolled over and over on the ground. At last, the Mohican's knife went into Magua's back. Magua fell over and lay still.

Chingachgook got to his feet, a smile on his face. But just then, Magua jumped up and got away into the woods.

"He tricked us!" Hawkeye cried. "The coward! Well, let him go. He is only one man and he has no rifle."

Uncas ran over to the girls. He took the ropes off Alice and placed her in her sister's arms.

Hawkeye cut the ropes off David. "Now, listen to me!" he said to the singing teacher. "Buy a rifle and work with it until you are a good shot. Then, the next time there is danger, you will be of some use."

David held out his thin hand to Hawkeye. "Friend," he said, "thank you for saving me."

Smiling, Duncan walked up to the two men. "That goes for me, too," he said to Hawkeye. "But I have been wondering. Why did you not go to Fort William Henry for help?"

"It would have come too late," Hawkeye answered. "You would have been dead before we could get back. As soon as we got some rifle powder, we trailed you. That way, when you needed us, we were ready."

After resting and eating, they started off for Fort William Henry. By hurrying, they covered a good many miles before the sun set. That night, they went as fast as they could in the dark.

They rode many miles without saying a word. Then Hawkeye held up his hand for them to stop. "Be quiet!" he said. "I hear a man coming our way."

The men brought up their rifles, ready to fire. Wide-eyed, Alice and Cora put their hands to their mouths.

Then, a man called out from the dark. He was French.

Putting his hand over Hawkeye's mouth, Duncan called an answer in French. The man talked with Duncan for some time and then left.

"That was close," Duncan said. "I was not sure I could get away with it. He was a French soldier. I told him we were French, too. He told me to be careful because there were English soldiers in the woods. He said General Montcalm and his soldiers are in front of Fort William Henry. They are right by the lake."

Hawkeye smiled at Duncan. "It is a good thing you were with us. I don't know French."

"But what are we going to do?" asked Duncan. "The French are between us and the fort."

Hawkeye thought, rubbing his head. "We must go up in the hills," he said. "We can hide there."

"Let's do that—and fast," said Duncan.

It was not long before they came to the foot of a large hill. The climb up was hard work. The horses kept sliding. The girls had to hold on to the horses' necks to keep from falling off.

By morning they were up high enough to see for miles around. To each side, there were big hills, one after another. The hills looked blue in the morning light. In front of them was mile after mile of dark green woods. On the other side of the woods, facing Lake Erie, stood the buildings of Fort William Henry.

In front of the fort were the white tents of General Montcalm's French soldiers.

"How many soldiers does Montcalm have?" Duncan asked in surprise. "There are so many tents."

"Look!" Cora cried. From where she stood, she could see her father's house in the fort. "A shot just hit the side of my father's house. I can not

bear to be here when he is in such danger. Take me to General Montcalm! He will let a child go through his lines to her father."

Hawkeye looked down at her and smiled. "You never know what the French might do," he said. "But there may be a way to get through their lines. This is lake country and the fog will be rolling in soon. The French will not see us in the fog. If we move fast and keep quiet, we might get through their lines. But you ladies will have to go on foot. Do you think you can do it?"

"Just watch us," Cora said. "Let's get started!"

They found climbing down the hill as hard as going up. The girls had to be helped at every step of the way. By the time they got to the bottom, a heavy, wet fog had rolled in. They could not see more than a few feet. Now they had to stay close together so no one would get lost.

After walking for some time, they heard some French soldiers talking. The soldiers did not see them through the fog.

But then, one of the soldiers heard their steps. He cried out and the soldiers began firing into the fog.

The shells cut through the heavy fog, almost

hitting the girls. They kept quiet, but they were so afraid they were shaking.

One by one, the soldiers stopped firing. They listened for steps, but heard nothing. They started talking to each other again.

Hawkeye waited a few minutes before starting off again. His party followed him through the heavy fog for almost a mile. Then Alice fell, making a loud noise.

Not far in front of them, a voice called out in English, "Stand ready! As soon as you see the enemy, fire!"

The girls knew that voice. "Father! Father!" cried Alice. "Please don't fire."

"Hold your fire!" came the answer. "It is Alice!"

Hawkeye had brought the girls home. But there was no time to talk. The French began to attack the fort. Colonel Munro sent the girls inside where they would be out of danger. Then he and Duncan hurried off to their men.

# 6 A Red Coat

The fighting went on for many days. The English soldiers were putting up a good fight. But there were not enough men or rifles.

Not far away were some more English soldiers. General Webb was in command of them. Colonel Munro sent Hawkeye to tell General Webb that the fort needed help.

But Hawkeye was caught trying to get back through the French lines. The French were holding him captive.

Duncan heard about Hawkeye from Colonel Munro himself. "General Montcalm sent word that he has a letter for me," said Colonel Munro. "He took it from Hawkeye. So, it must be from General Webb."

"Colonel Munro," Duncan said, "we can not hold the fort for long. Many of our rifles will not fire. We are short of powder and food, too. And each day there are more wounded and dead."

The Colonel said, "As long as there is any hope, we will hold this fort. Powder or no powder. But I don't know if General Webb and his men are coming. I must get that letter."

"Can I help in some way?" asked Duncan.

"Yes, Major Heyward, you can." Colonel Munro placed his hands behind his back, walking as he talked. "General Montcalm wants me to go over to his camp for a talk. But I am needed here. Please, go in my place. And get that letter!"

In ten minutes, Duncan was walking toward the French camp. He was carrying a white flag. When he came to the camp, the French soldiers took him to their General.

General Montcalm was very kind to Duncan. But he would not give him General Webb's letter. He told Duncan that he would give the letter only to Colonel Munro.

When Colonel Munro heard what General Montcalm said, he was angry. "So, he will talk only to me. Well, we must have that letter. Send word that I will meet him. I will go right away."

It was late afternoon when Colonel Munro came back from the French camp. His step was heavy and he looked sad. He waited until he and Duncan were alone. Then he said, "General Webb is not coming!"

"You saw the letter?" Duncan asked.

"Yes," Colonel Munro told him. "I almost wish I had not. The letter went on for three pages. But all it said was that the General and his men were not coming. Duncan, my boy, we must face Montcalm alone."

Colonel Munro sat down, covering his face with his hands. "What is the right thing to do?" he asked. "I don't want to give up the fort. But what about the women and children? And what about my men?"

That night there was another meeting between General Montcalm and Colonel Munro. The

General said he only wanted the fort. If the Colonel would give up the fort, the English could march away. No one would be hurt. The English soldiers could even keep their rifles and their flag.

Colonel Munro did not like it. But he knew dead men were of no use to his King. And he could not bear to put the women and children in danger. He told General Montcalm that he could have the fort in the morning.

Fort William Henry was very busy the next morning. The English were getting ready to leave. Colonel Munro came up to Duncan. "Major Heyward," he said, "I must help all of the women and children get ready. I have no time for my own children. Will you look after them?"

He did not have to say anything else. Duncan hurried over to Cora and Alice. Alice was crying. Cora was sad, but she gave Duncan a sweet smile.

"I must see that you are cared for," said Duncan.

"We will be all right, Duncan," said Cora. "You must march with your men. We will follow and try to help the mothers with their children."

"But it is a long, hard march," Duncan said. "You will need a man to help you on the way."

Duncan heard a man singing. He knew of only one man who would sing at a time like this. Coming toward him was David Gamut.

"Hello, David," said Duncan, taking hold of the singing teacher's arm. "Will you please watch after Cora and Alice on the march? The Colonel and I must stay with our men."

A smile came over David's thin face. "I'll be glad to help the young ladies," he said. "I'll sing to them along the way."

Duncan watched as David helped the two girls. He would have felt better taking care of them himself.

At last, it was time to leave the fort. The English soldiers marched out first. The women and children followed them. Then, the French took over Fort William Henry.

The march was slow going for the English. The little children could not walk fast. Their mothers had to carry them or pull them along. Even the soldiers had a hard time of it. Many of them were wounded. And all of them were tired.

The English had not gone far when Magua

and his Hurons came from the woods. The Indians made no sound. They stood as still as the trees behind them. Only their eyes moved. The Hurons watched the soldiers march by and go into the woods.

Then, as the women and children were going by, something happened. An Indian saw a red coat that a little girl was carrying. He ran up to the child and grabbed her coat. But the little girl would not let go. She tried to pull her coat away from the Indian. With an angry yell, the Indian dropped the coat and grabbed the child.

The little girl's mother cried out, "No! You can have the coat. Give me back my child!"

The Indian looked at the woman and laughed. Swinging the child by her legs, he hit her little head against a rock. Then he threw the dead child at her mother's feet.

When Magua saw this, he gave a wild war cry. The Hurons attacked.

Afraid and crying the women tried to escape with their children. But they were knifed, tomahawked, and shot as they ran. In minutes, blood was all over the ground.

The English soldiers heard the noise and turned back. But the French had not let them

take powder for their rifles. So the English had to fight the Indians with their hands.

David was trying to get Alice and Cora away. But Alice had fainted.

"Run, David!" cried Cora. "Run while there is still time." She looked down at her sister. "I must stay with Alice."

In his own way, David was a brave man. "I am staying, too," he said. "I will try to quiet the Indians."

While the Hurons were yelling, killing, and scalping, David began to sing. His song did not quiet the Hurons. But it did catch the ear of one Indian—Magua. Magua saw David. And he saw Cora standing beside him.

Magua pushed his way through the fighting to Cora. "Come," he said. "The tent of the Huron is still open. Is it not better than this?"

"Get away from me!" cried Cora.

Magua saw Alice on the ground. He picked her up in his arms and ran toward the woods.

Without thinking, Cora followed him. "Put my sister down!" she cried.

David tried to stop Cora. But she pushed him away and ran on. David followed her. He knew he could not do much against the Indians. But he had to try.

Magua carried Alice to where he had left two horses. He threw Alice across one of the horses.

Cora ran up and tried to pull her sister off the horse. But Magua pushed her away.

Pointing to another horse, he said, "If you want, come. If not, your sister will live in Magua's tent."

Then, Magua jumped on the horse behind Alice. Whipping the horse, he rode into the woods. He did not even look behind him. He knew that Cora would come after her sister.

It took Cora a few minutes to get on the other horse. By that time, David came running up. He climbed up behind Cora on the horse. Then, the two of them took off after Magua and Alice.

# 7 On the Trail

Hawkeye, Uncas, and Chingachgook had been captives of the French. It was late in the afternoon when the French let them go. Now, the three of them were standing near the woods in front of the fort. Dead English soldiers and women and children lay everyplace. They were used to seeing soliders killed in war. But seeing so many women and children like this made them feel sick.

As they looked over the field of dead, two men came toward them. They were Colonel Munro and Duncan Heyward. Both men had been knocked out and left for dead by the Hurons. Now, they were walking around looking for some sign of Cora and Alice.

"Where are my children?" cried Colonel Munro as he came up to Hawkeye. "Where are my little girls?"

"I don't know," answered Hawkeye. "But we are going to find out."

Just then, Uncas saw something. He yelled and raced over to a tree. A piece of Cora's dress was caught on a branch! The young Mohican hunted for more signs of a trail. The other men followed him into the woods.

The five men followed the trail the rest of the day. They spent the night by the lake. This was country that even Hawkeye thought of as wild. He was the only white man who had ever been there before.

Next morning, Hawkeye called the others around him. "It must be Magua who has the girls," he said. "Their trail is going north. Magua should stay between the lake and the river. If our thinking is right, we will cross their trail soon. Let's get going!"

Uncas gave each tree they came to a careful going over. He looked at the ground in front of him before taking each step. Sometimes he felt the ground or a rock with his hand.

Magua had used all the tricks he knew to cover his trail. But Uncas saw through them all. That afternoon, the young Mohican found a place where a man had walked.

"White man," Uncas said.

Hawkeye looked to where Uncas was pointing. "No Indian made that," he said.

"David Gamut!" said Duncan. "He was with the girls. It must be David."

They pushed on. The trail was better now. They could make better time.

By late afternoon, Colonel Munro was very tired. The old man had a hard time keeping up with the other men. Only the thought of Alice and Cora kept him going. He was glad when Hawkeye stopped.

"I smell Hurons," Hawkeye said. "The woods end not far from here. From then on we will be in open country. Let's do a little scouting. Uncas, you go to the left. Chingachgook, try that hill. I'll follow the trail. If anything happens, give a bird call—three times."

The Mohicans left without saying a word. Colonel Munro dropped to the ground to rest. But Duncan could not rest. He went with Hawkeye. They had not gone far when Duncan saw a man off to his left. Duncan could see only the man's back. Like the Mohicans, he had almost no hair on his head. And in what hair he had were some feathers.

"Hawkeye!" said Duncan. "On my left! An Indian."

Hawkeye looked where Duncan was pointing. "He is no Huron," Hawkeye said. "I don't know what he is. I thought I knew every tribe in this part of the world."

All at once, Hawkeye started laughing. "I think I know after all! Stay here. I'll go get him."

Hawkeye was not gone long. Soon he was back with the man Duncan thought was an Indian. It was David Gamut!

"Well, Mr. Gamut," said Hawkeye, still laughing. "Are you busy teaching the birds to sing?"

Hawkeye put his hands to his mouth. He gave three bird calls. Soon the Mohicans and Colonel Munro came running up the trail.

Colonel Munro's eyes grew bright when he saw David. "Where are Cora and Alice?" he called. "How are my children?"

David waited until the Colonel was close before answering. "They are tired and afraid," he said. "But they have not been hurt."

"Why do the Hurons let you come and go as you please?" Duncan asked. "Why don't they keep you tied up?"

"Because I sing to them," said David, smiling. "My singing makes these wild men kind to me."

Hawkeye laughed. "In a way he is right," he said. "I think his singing made the Hurons think him crazy. Indians never hurt a crazy man. They think he has been visited by the Great Spirit."

Then Hawkeye turned to David. "And Magua?" he asked. "What of him?"

"He went hunting today," said David. "I don't know when he will be back."

"My girls, where are they?" Colonel Munro asked.

"Cora was sent to another tribe," David

answered. "She is not too far away. The tribe lives over there." David pointed to the hills behind Colonel Munro. "They are said to be enemies of the English," he told Hawkeye.

"Did you see any pictures of the turtle on their tents?" Hawkeye asked. "Like this." He pointed to Chingachgook's back. On the Mohican's back was a picture of a blue turtle.

"Yes! Yes!" said David, surprised. "I saw many pictures just like that."

"They are Delaware," Hawkeye told him. "That may be a help. Once Chingachgook and the chief of the Delaware were like brothers. They both follow the sign of the turtle. Cora is better off with them than with the Hurons."

"Is there any way I can help?" asked David.

"Yes," said Hawkeye. "Go back to the Huron camp. Find out what they are planning to do with the girls. When you hear my bird call, come back here."

"I am going with him," said Duncan.

"Are you tired of living?" asked Hawkeye.

"But the Hurons did not kill David," Duncan pointed out.

"That is because they think he is crazy," said Hawkeye. "With you, it will be another story."

"I am going, Hawkeye," said Duncan. "And nothing can stop me."

Hawkeye threw his hands up in the air. "All right! All right! If we paint you up like a magician, they may not kill you. But don't count on it."

Chingachgook brought out the little bag of paints Indians always carried. He painted Duncan's face. But he was careful not to paint any war signs. He painted Duncan to look like an Indian magician.

When Chingachgook had finished, Hawkeye put his hand on Duncan's arm. "I'll say this much for you," he said. "You are no coward. But you are going to have to use your head. You will be in great danger every minute you are in the Huron camp. You know what they will do to you if they find out who you are."

The Huron camp was not far away. Before Duncan and David had walked a mile, they saw the first Huron tent. Four braves ran out to meet them. Without saying a word, they dragged Duncan to the tent of their chief.

The Huron chief was sitting on the ground. He was smoking and talking to some other Indians. He looked Duncan over. Then he asked, "What are you doing here?"

"The great French white father sent me to his children," Duncan answered. "I am to help those who are sick. I am a great magician."

The chief looked as if he did not believe Duncan. "We scalped those English women and children," he said. "Is not the French white father angry?"

Duncan made himself smile. "The English

are his enemies," he said. "The white father is happy."

"Why does the white magician paint his face?" asked the chief. His voice was cold.

"When an Indian visits his white brothers, he wears white man's clothes," said Duncan. He made a point of looking straight into the chief's eyes. "So, when I visit you, I paint my face."

Duncan's answer pleased the Hurons. Even the chief smiled. Just then, a wild war cry was heard. The Hurons ran out of the tent to see what was happening. Duncan followed them.

The cry had come from a Huron war party. They were coming into the camp with two Indian captives.

The captives' hands were tied behind their backs. As they came into the camp, all the Hurons began hitting them.

One of the captives cried out with each blow. Then he fell to the ground, crying. A Huron brave pulled out his knife and killed him.

"Coward!" said the brave, cleaning his knife on the dead man's arm.

The other captive had not made a sound. Head up, he looked straight in front of him. And he took the blows as if he did not feel them. As he came near, Duncan saw his face. It was Uncas!

# 8 The Bear

The Hurons were getting ready to make Uncas run the Race of the Captives. Few men have ever lived through it.

For the race, the Hurons stood in two lines. Each brave was armed with a stone, a knife, or a tomahawk. Uncas would have to run between these two lines of armed men. They were going to try to kill him as he ran. If he got to the end, they would stop hitting him. But the Hurons felt sure they could kill Uncas before he finished the race. The chief gave the sign to begin.

Duncan did not think Uncas could make it. Before he had run five steps, he was covered with blood. Once he was knifed by a Huron and fell. Duncan thought he had been killed. But he jumped to his feet. Blood was coming out of a leg wound, but he kept running.

The Huron standing next to Duncan began swinging his tomahawk as Uncas neared them. But just as he threw it, Duncan bumped into him. The tomahawk missed. Uncas ran by and made the end of the lines.

The blows and yelling stopped. But the quiet
was heavy and angry. A brave pushed Uncas
into the chief's tent.

As Duncan was trying to think of some way to help, the chief saw him. "Come," he said, taking Duncan into the tent. "One of my sons is sick. Our magician is not making him well. Can you make my son well?"

"Yes," said Duncan. "I'll soon have your son sitting by your side."

As he talked, Duncan heard a noise behind him. The chief looked up and smiled.

"Did Magua have good hunting?" the chief asked.

Magua had just come into the tent. He was about to answer when he spotted Uncas. "Mohican!" Magua cried in surprise.

He turned to the chief. "This is my great enemy. Let Magua kill him."

Magua began swinging his tomahawk over his head. Then he stopped. "No," he said. "Magua will kill his enemy in the morning. Sleep well, Mohican!"

Magua looked at his chief. The chief made a sign. Two Hurons grabbed Uncas and dragged him from the tent behind Magua.

After they left, a large black bear walked into the tent. Pointing to the bear, the chief said, "This is our magician. He will take you to my son. If he is not well by morning, you will be killed with the Mohican." Then, the chief and the other Hurons left the tent.

Duncan found himself alone with the bear. He knew Indians often kept bears for pets. But he wondered why the chief had said the bear was a magician.

The bear walked toward Duncan. Duncan backed away. But the bear caught hold of his leg with its paw. Duncan was afraid to move. He watched as the bear grabbed its own head and started pulling at it. All at once, the bear's head came off! In its place Duncan saw Hawkeye's smiling face.

"But—but—I thought you were a real bear," said Duncan.

Hawkeye laughed. "I was afraid you would run away before I could get the head off."

"*You* were afraid!" It was Duncan's turn to laugh. "Thank God you are here! But what are you doing in the bear?"

"Coming after you and Uncas," said Hawkeye. "This skin belongs to the tribe magician. I knocked him out and took it. I can go where I please in it. Even the chief is a little afraid of the magician."

"What can we do?" Duncan asked. "Magua is going to kill Uncas in the morning."

"We will see about that," Hawkeye said. "But first, let's get Alice out of here. I know where she is. But I don't want to go to her in this skin. She would be so afraid that she might faint. You go to her. But rub the paint off your face first. Then she can see who you are.

Hawkeye pulled Duncan to the tent's opening and pointed out. "See that tent with the sun painted on it?" he said. "Alice is in there. Get her ready to escape. I'll scout around for the best way out of the camp."

Duncan ran to Alice's tent. When she saw him, Alice started crying. "I did not think I would ever see you again," she said.

Duncan put his arms around Alice and held her close. But then he felt a tap on his back. He turned his head and found Magua standing behind him.

"So, Magua finds the white soldier in his captive's tent," the Huron said. "Now Magua can find out how white men like to be whipped."

Magua brought up his hand to hit Duncan. But just then, the Huron was caught and held from behind. Hawkeye, still inside the bear, had come into the tent. The scout knocked Magua out.

Alice had fainted when Magua was about to hit Duncan. But the men could not wait until she came to. Any minute now another Huron might come into the tent. So, Duncan picked her up in his arms and carried her. He followed Hawkeye out of the tent. They went down a back trail, away from the Huron camp.

Alice was soon feeling better. "I think I can walk now," she told Duncan.

"Good," said Hawkeye, "because I must go back and help Uncas escape. You know what they will do to him if I don't. You two go to the camp of the Delawares. Colonel Munro and Chingachgook are hiding near there. I don't know if Uncas and I can escape. But if we do, we will meet you at the camp of the Delawares."

Alice and Duncan watched the scout run back along the trail. They were afraid they would never see him again.

# 9 A Trick

Hawkeye headed back to the Huron camp. He was still inside the magician's bear. When he came to the camp, no one tried to stop him. The Indians were a little afraid of the tribe's magician. They thought he was inside the skin.

As he was going by one tent, Hawkeye heard singing. It was David Gamut. Hawkeye went into the singing teacher's tent.

David was afraid when he saw the bear. "Go away!" he cried. He jumped up and began to sing. He was hoping to make the bear leave.

"Don't be afraid, David," laughed Hawkeye. He pulled off the bear's head. "It is only me inside the magician's bear. I am going to help Uncas escape. Will you help me?"

"Yes," said David, still shaking. "I'll take you to his tent. But how will we get Uncas away? His tent is being watched by five Huron braves."

"We will have to trick them," answered Hawkeye. Then he put on the bear's head again. "You tell the braves that the magician wants to visit the Mohican. I'll do the rest."

When they saw David and the bear coming, the five braves stood up. "The magician comes to see the captive," David said. "Let him go in!"

The braves moved away from the front of the tent. One brave made a sign for the bear to go in. But the bear just sat down and waved his paws. Then he gave a loud roar.

"He will not go in while you are standing there," said David. "Go away!"

The Hurons looked angry. But they were afraid of the magician. They moved away. Then the bear got up and went into the tent. David stayed outside to keep watch.

Uncas was tied up in one corner of the tent. Hawkeye gave a fierce roar as he walked toward him. He wanted the braves outside to hear it. But Uncas was not afraid. He did not even look up at the bear. Then Hawkeye made another noise. It sounded like a bee buzzing.

Uncas looked up. His eyes were shining. "Hawkeye!" he cried. "Is that you inside the bear?"

Hawkeye made another buzzing noise. Then he took off the skin.

"Cut his ropes," he said to David, who had just come in.

"How are we going to escape?" asked David. "The five Hurons are not far away."

"Quick, Uncas," said Hawkeye, "get inside the bear. David, give me your clothes. I will look enough like you in the dark that no one will stop us."

"But what about me?" David asked.

"Lie down," said Hawkeye. "It is dark in here. The Hurons will think you are Uncas when they look in. They will not find you for a while. By then, we can be at the camp of the Delawares. When the Hurons do find you, start singing. They think you are crazy, so they will not hurt you. As soon as you can, come to the camp of the Delawares."

Hawkeye and Uncas left the tent. Hawkeye was in David's clothes. Uncas was inside the magician's bear. The Hurons came toward them. Just as they came close, Uncas let out a fierce roar. Afraid, the Hurons backed away. Uncas and Hawkeye went right by them and headed toward the woods. Hawkeye began to sing. He was trying to sound like David.

The five braves watched them go. Then they went over and sat down in front of the tent again. After a few minutes, one brave stood up. He went inside the tent and walked over to the captive. When he saw David, he let out an angry yell. "The Mohican has escaped!" he cried as he ran from the tent.

The five braves ran from tent to tent, waking the tribe. Soon the camp was full of noise.

Magua called the angry braves to him. "Hurry! After the Mohican!" he yelled.

Magua did not take the time to trail Uncas. He was sure Uncas would go after Cora. So, he took his men straight to the Delawares' camp.

The sun was coming up as the Hurons came into the camp. Uncas and Hawkeye were already there. Magua was surprised to find that Duncan and Alice were also in the camp. But he was glad they were all there together. Now, he thought, I can get the Delawares to hand over all my enemies.

But old Chief Tamenund of the Delawares knew more than most men. When he looked at a man, he knew what that man was thinking. Chief Tamenund had never liked Magua. He knew that the Huron was a coward. But Magua was a chief of the Hurons. And the Hurons were the Delawares' friends. So, he had to listen to Magua.

Magua had a plan to trick Chief Tamenund. Part of his trick was to make the chief think he was angry. He walked up to the chief and cried, "I have come for the dark-haired woman. But I find my enemies in your tent. That one is an English scout." Magua pointed to Hawkeye. "He has killed Delaware braves as well as Hurons." Then Magua pointed to Uncas. "This one is his friend. They are your enemies. You should kill them."

Three Delaware braves did not wait to hear more. Before their chief could stop them, they grabbed Uncas. But in doing so, they pulled the clothes off his back. With a cry of surprise, the braves let Uncas go. They had seen the blue turtle on his back.

Chief Tamenund stood up. "Who are you to have this sign on your back?" he cried.

"Uncas, the son of Chingachgook," the young Mohican answered.

The Delaware chief walked over and put his hand on Uncas' arm. He looked into the young Mohican's eyes. "Is it really so?" he asked. "Uncas, the son of Chingachgook! Your grandfather's father and I were as brothers when we were boys. You and your father are the last chiefs of the Turtle. Until this minute, I thought you were dead. It is a good day that brought Uncas, the son of Chingachgook, to my tent."

Uncas put his hand on the old chief's arm. "Chief Tamenund," he said, "do not kill Hawkeye. He is my friend."

"You should not call Hawkeye a friend," said Chief Tamenund. "Magua says he has killed many of my young braves."

Hawkeye stepped up to the old chief and looked him in the eye. "I have killed many Hurons, but not one Delaware brave," he said. "He that says I ever hurt a Delaware lies."

Chief Tamenund's eyes moved to where Magua stood. "Then has the Huron been lying to me?" he asked.

"Tamenund is a just chief as well as a great one," said Magua. "He will not keep what belongs to me. These white people and the Mohican belong to me."

The old chief turned again to Uncas. "Tell me what is right," he said. "Are you Magua's captive?"

Uncas answered by shaking his head.

"And Hawkeye," Tamenund went on, "is he Magua's captive?"

Uncas laughed. "No. Just ask the Hurons who has their magician's bear."

"And the soldier and the woman who came into my camp together?" asked Tamenund.

"They made good their escape from the Huron camp," said Uncas.

"And the dark-haired woman?"

Uncas dropped his eyes and did not answer.

"She belongs to me," Magua cried. "Mohican, you know that is so."

"My son does not answer," the old chief said in a soft voice.

At last Uncas had to say, "It is so. She is his captive."

Chief Tamenund was sad. He wanted to help the son of his old friend. But he was a chief. He had to be just and follow the ways of his people. Then he had a thought. "Let me give you money for the dark-haired woman," he said.

"No!" said Magua. "It is not money I want."

Shaking his head, Tamenund said, "Then take what is yours and go."

"Stop!" Hawkeye cried. He walked up to Magua. "Take me in place of the woman. Do with me as you like. But let her go."

Magua stopped for a minute. He longed to stick a knife into his enemy. But he hated Colonel Munro even more than he hated Hawkeye. He wanted to get even with the Colonel by taking Cora. Magua pulled Cora away. "Magua will keep the woman," he said.

"Huron!" cried Uncas. "Look at the sun. When it can be seen over the trees, I will be on your trail."

Chief Tamenund faced Magua. "I did what I had to do," he said. "But the enemy of the Mohicans is the enemy of the Delawares. My young braves will go with Uncas."

"I am not afraid," said Magua. He turned his back on the chief and dragged Cora from the tent.

Once Magua was out of their camp, the Delawares got ready for war.

# 10 The Last of the Mohicans

The Delaware war party was heading for the Huron camp. Hawkeye and Uncas were in command.

"I'll take my braves and go to the right," said Hawkeye. "I'll pick up Chingachgook and Colonel Munro on the way. Your braves will go toward the Huron camp on the left, Uncas. Attack when you hear my call. We will go at them from both sides. Then we will catch them between us."

"A good plan!" cried Duncan. "I will go with you, Hawkeye."

Uncas told the braves the plan of attack. Then Hawkeye and his men went off to the right. Uncas and his men went to the left. They moved through the woods like deer.

Hawkeye and his Delawares did not go far, though, before the Hurons spotted them. A rifle barked, and one of Hawkeye's braves fell dead.

"Take cover!" cried Hawkeye.

The Delawares ran behind trees. Using the trees for cover, they fired back at the Hurons.

Then, yelling and firing, they ran from tree to tree toward the Hurons.

The Delawares were good fighting men. But they were fighting on the Hurons' home ground. There were two Hurons for every Delaware. Things were not going well for the Delawares.

Just then, the Hurons were attacked from the other side. Uncas had heard the rifle fire. He had not waited for Hawkeye's call.

Chingachgook and Colonel Munro had heard the firing, too. They ran to help the attack.

The Hurons were surprised. Some of them ran away. The others fell back to their camp.

Uncas and Hawkeye brought their braves together. With tomahawks swinging, the Delawares moved in on the Huron camp. The ground was covered with the dead and wounded. War cries and yells filled the air.

Magua saw that the fight was lost. Taking one Huron brave with him, he ran to Cora's tent. He dragged Cora from the tent. There was a hill on the far side of the Huron camp. Once he was over the hill, thought Magua, he could escape. Grabbing Cora's arm, he pulled her up the hill.

But Uncas had seen them. "Cora! Cora!" he yelled, running after them. Hawkeye followed him.

Cora heard Uncas' voice. "You can not make me take one more step," she said to Magua.

Magua pulled out his scalping knife. "Is it going to be Magua's tent or Magua's knife? Which do you want?

Before Cora could answer, Magua saw Uncas. The young Mohican was flying head first at Magua.

85

Magua jumped away. But the other Huron grabbed Cora and killed her with his knife.

Uncas had missed Magua. Before he could get up, Magua knifed him in the back. Then he started running up the hill to get away.

Blood running from his wound, Uncas got to his feet. With one blow of his tomahawk, he killed the brave who had knifed Cora. Then he fell dead at Cora's side.

Now that there was no danger of hitting Cora or Uncas, Hawkeye fired his rifle. Just before Magua got to the top of the hill, the scout shot him dead.

*         *         *

It was a sad war party that went back to the Delawares' camp. Though the sun was bright, the day seemed dark. They carried Cora and Uncas with them.

Alice fainted when she learned that Cora had been killed. When she came to, Colonel Munro tried to tell her what had happened. But he could not find the words.

Chief Tamenund and his tribe did everything they could to help. They had come to love the dark-haired girl and the young Mohican.

Cora was buried near a tall, beautiful tree on a little hill. Alice and the Delaware girls covered the ground with flowers. The Delawares sang their song of the dead over her. Then David Gamut sang his own good-by to Cora.

"There is nothing more we can do here," said Colonel Munro to Duncan. "We had better leave now." He walked up to Chief Tamenund. "Thank you for being kind to my children," he said. "Thank you . . . . " He wanted to say more, but he could not.

Duncan helped Alice get on her horse. He rode on one side of her, and David rode on the other side. Colonel Munro headed the party. Chief Tamenund sent two braves to show them the way through the woods. Colonel Munro turned for a last look at the tree near Cora. Then he started off along the trail.

When it came time to bury Uncas, Chingachgook looked at his dead son. "Why have you left us, hope of the Mohicans?" he cried. "Who that saw you fight would believe you would be killed? In all the world there was no one like you. And now that you are gone, there is no one to take your place. I am alone in the world."

Hawkeye went over to his old friend. He put his hand on the Mohican's arm. "No, Mohican, you are not alone," he said. "He was your son, but I loved him, too. We will walk the same trail, you and I. He has left us, but you are not alone, Chingachgook."

Chief Tamenund was shaking his head. "I have lived too many days," he said. "This morning the son of Chingachgook was strong. Now I must bury him. The Turtles have lost another chief. The last young brave of the Mohicans is dead."